KU-511-687

PUB TRIVIA QUIZ

LAGOON BOOKS, LONDON

Series Editor: Simon Melhuish
Editor: Heather Dickson
Page design and layout: Linley Clode
Cover design: James Davies

Published by:
LAGOON BOOKS
PO BOX 311, KT2 5QW, UK

ISBN 1-89971-250-X

PUB TRIVIA QUIZ

LAGOON BOOKS, LONDON

This book contains some of the wildest, wackiest and down-right ridiculous trivia relating to booze and boozing ever assembled in one place. It quite simply makes for an excellent read, but if you're the competitive sort you can ...

HOST YOUR OWN PUB TRIVIA QUIZ

The question pages are all in colour, and are numbered. The corresponding answer pages are in black and white, and immediately follow each question page — they are also numbered accordingly.

The numbers on the page edge (2, 4, 6, 8 & 10) refer to the point value that is scored for a correct answer and reflect the relative ease or difficulty of the question.

Players form two or more teams, and a question master is appointed. The question master chooses a question page at random, ensures that everyone is aware that he is about to read a 'starter' question (worth 2 points), and reads out the first question on the page.

Each team has already been allotted a 'buzzer' sound — the

more ridiculous the sound the better. The first team to 'buzz' after the question has been read out is allowed to answer all the questions on the page.

SCORING

Each correct answer scores the point value next to the question. Each incorrect answer loses half the point value of the question. All incorrectly answered questions are handed over to the opposition in an even-handed manner. They score half the point value for a correct answer and nothing for an incorrect answer.

The 'buzz' team (who are answering all the questions on the page) can choose to pass on any question — but then the opposing teams score the full point value if correct, and lose nothing if incorrect.

The question master keeps score, and has the final decision in any disputes. It is quite possible that all teams will have minus scores — in which case it is still the team with the highest score (nearest to zero) that wins! *HAVE FUN!*

1 — Questions

In sign language, whisky is indicated by two fingers poked down the throat. True or false?

What is a 'dew drink'?
- **A** A drink before breakfast
- **B** A drink made with rainwater
- **C** A weak drink

What is a 'sconce'?
- **A** An Oxford University beer challenge
- **B** A small, semi-private room in an English pub
- **C** A loud boorish drunk

Who plays the bartender on the U.S.S Enterprise in "Star Trek: The Next Generation"?

According to P.J. O'Rourke, what is the only rule at the Commodore Bar in Beirut?

The word 'inebriated' stems from the Latin 'embrace' meaning 'to shine like the moon'. True or false?

2

Glen Turret, Scotland's oldest distillery dates from...
- **A** 1243
- **B** 1576
- **C** 1775

4

Which Shakespearean hero said: "I would give all my fame for a pot of ale and safety."?

6

In the "Hitchhikers Guide to the Galaxy", what is the name of the dangerously strong drink favoured by Zaphod Beeblebrox and Ford Prefect?

8

Which American singer/songwriter has written songs such as "Jockey Full of Bourbon", "Gin Soaked Boy" and "The Piano Has Been Drinking, Not Me", and has played barmen in two Francis Ford Coppola films and a dying hobo alongside Jack Nicholson?

10

2 > *In sign language, whisky is indicated by two fingers poked down the throat. True or false?*
False

4 > *What is a 'dew drink'?*
A A drink before breakfast

6 > *What is a 'sconce'?*
A An Oxford University beer challenge

8 > *Who plays the bartender on the U.S.S Enterprise in "Star Trek: The Next Generation"?*
Whoopi Goldberg

10 > *According to P.J. O'Rourke, what is the only rule at the Commodore Bar in Beirut?*
No guns

The word 'inebriated' stems from the Latin 'embrare' meaning 'to shine like the moon'. True or false?

2

   False

Glen Turret, Scotland's oldest distillery dates from...

4

   C 1775

Which Shakespearean hero said: "I would give all my fame for a pot of ale and safety."?

6

   Henry V

In the "Hitchhikers Guide to the Galaxy", what is the name of the dangerously strong drink favoured by Zaphod Beeblebrox and Ford Prefect?

8

   The Pan Galactic Gargle Blaster

Which American singer/songwriter has written songs such as "Jockey Full of Bourbon", "Gin Soaked Boy" and "The Piano Has Been Drinking, Not Me", and has played barmen in two Francis Ford Coppola films and a dying hobo alongside Jack Nicholson?

10

   Tom Waits

According to Dean Martin, you're not drunk if you can...

2

A Remember who you are

B Lie on the floor without holding on

C Tie your tie, button your fly and remember which way is down

---

Is ale with a dash of gin known as...

4

A A Cat Call

B A Cod's Wallop

C A Dog's Nose

Oscar Levant said: "I don't drink liquor. I don't like it. It...

6

A ...makes me feel good."

B ...makes me act like my father and think like my mother."

C ...makes my feet bigger and the sidewalk smaller."

8

What is the origin of 'chunder', meaning to vomit?

10

What happened for the last time in England on 11 June 1872, to drunkard Mark Tuck, as a result of him being an "incorrigible bacchanalian"?

From which country does the word 'grog' come?

2

During WW1, UK Prime Minister Lloyd George said:
"Drink is doing us more damage than all the _____
put together."
A Powdered eggs
B German submarines
C Americans

4

Where does "Let us eat and drink, for tomorrow we die,"
come from?
A "Henry V" by William Shakespeare
B "The Old Man and the Sea" by Ernest Hemingway
C The Book of Isaiah, in the Old Testament

6

What was the name of the invisible six-foot rabbit who
accompanied James Stewart's alcoholic millionaire
everywhere in the film of the same name?

8

Which American novelist observed: "first you take a drink,
then the drink takes a drink, then the drink takes you."?

10

2 | *According to Dean Martin, you're not drunk if you can...*
B Lie on the floor without holding on

4 | *Is ale with a dash of gin known as...*
C A Dog's Nose

6 | *Oscar Levant said: "I don't drink liquor. I don't like it. It...*
A ...makes me feel good."

8 | *What is the origin of 'chunder', meaning to vomit?*
If someone was sick over the side on the Australian prison ships, they'd shout "Watch under!" which was reduced to 'chunder'

10 | *What happened for the last time in England on 11 June 1872, to drunkard Mark Tuck, as a result of him being an "incorrigible bacchanalian"?*
He was put in the stocks

From which country does the word 'grog' come?
Australia

2

During WW1, UK Prime Minister Lloyd George said:
"Drink is doing us more damage than all the _____
put together."
   B   German submarines

4

Where does "Let us eat and drink, for tomorrow we die,"
come from?
   C   The Book of Isaiah, in the Old Testament

6

What was the name of the invisible six-foot rabbit who
accompanied James Stewart's alcoholic millionaire
everywhere in the film of the same name?
Harvey

8

Which American novelist observed: "first you take a drink,
then the drink takes a drink, then the drink takes you."?
F. Scott Fitzgerald

10

2

Dionysus is the Roman god of fertility and wine.
True or false?

4

The expression "the real McCoy" comes from...
  A A Caribbean rum runner
  B An Irish whiskey advertising campaign from the 1890s
  C A special brew of Milwaukee "heavy"

6

According to legend, which ancient civilisation was taught
to brew beer by a god?
  A The Greeks
  B The Romans
  C The Egyptians

8

Which drink is mentioned in all of the following: "Death
of a Clown" (The Kinks), "Honky Tonk Women"
(The Rolling Stones) and "Substitute" (The Who)?

10

What is 'poteen'?

In semaphore, an alcoholic drink is represented by whirling one flag circularly about the head, whilst patting the stomach with the other. True or false?

2

What is a 'pundy'?
- **A** A beer belly
- **B** A free ration of beer for brewers
- **C** Enough beer to make you very drunk

4

In Australia, what drink is 'squatter's daughter' slang for?

6

What was the name of the creepy rural pub in "An American Werewolf in London"?

8

Which seventies hit mentions the "misty taste of moonshine"?

10

2

Dionysus is the Roman god of fertility and wine.
True or false?

False. He is the Greek god of fertility and wine

4

The expression "the real McCoy" comes from...

A A Caribbean rum runner

6

According to legend, which ancient civilisation was taught
to brew beer by a god?

C The Egyptians

8

Which drink is mentioned in all of the following: "Death
of a Clown" (The Kinks), "Honky Tonk Women"
(The Rolling Stones) and "Substitute" (The Who)?

Gin

10

What is 'poteen'?

Irish potato spirit

*In semaphore, an alcoholic drink is represented by
whirling one flag circularly about the head, whilst patting
the stomach with the other. True or false?*

> 2

False

What is a 'pundy'?

> 4

B A free ration of beer for brewers

---

*In Australia, what drink is 'squatter's daughter'
slang for?*

> 6

Water

---

*What was the name of the creepy rural pub in
"An American Werewolf in London"?*

> 8

The Slaughtered Lamb

---

*Which seventies hit mentions the "misty taste of
moonshine"?*

> 10

(Take Me Home) Country Roads, by John Denver

2   In America in 1790, an 'Anti Fogmatic' was an alcoholic drink supposed to counteract the bad effects of fog. True or false?

4   The walls of 'The Magdala' in Hampstead, North London, still show the bulletholes from a murder committed by...
- **A** Jack the Ripper
- **B** Ruth Ellis
- **C** Al Capone

6   In the grounds of Winchester Cathedral, a man is burried who, according to his gravestone, died from...
- **A** Drinking too much "small beer" on a hot day
- **B** Drinking cider after a "surfeit of young turnip"
- **C** Singing hymns heartily after consuming "an ill-fitting measure" of communion wine

8   In London, what do the areas of Swiss Cottage, Elephant & Castle and The Angel have in common?

10   If a spirit is 100 degrees proof, what is its percentage alcohol quantity?

Which city is considered to be the home of
American beer?

2

Traditionally Guinness is made with water from
which river?
- **A** The Shannon
- **B** The Moine
- **C** The Liffey

4

In Manitoba, Canada, where is drinking forbidden?
- **A** In church
- **B** In the toilet
- **C** In sight of under 16-year-olds and over 65s

6

What is the volume of a magnum?

8

How did Krook, the gin-drinking rag-and-bone man in
Charles Dickens' Bleak House meet his bizarre end?

10

2 In America in 1790, an 'Anti Fogmatic' was an alcoholic drink supposed to counteract the bad effects of fog. True or false?

True

4 The walls of 'The Magdala' in Hampstead, North London, still show the bulletholes from a murder committed by...

B Ruth Ellis

6 In the grounds of Winchester Cathedral, a man is burried who, according to his gravestone, died from...

A Drinking too much "small beer" on a hot day

8 In London, what do the areas of Swiss Cottage, Elephant & Castle and The Angel have in common?

They're all named after pubs

10 If a spirit is 100 degrees proof, what is its percentage alcohol quantity?

57.1%

Which city is considered to be the home of American beer? | 2
Milwaukee

Traditionally Guinness is made with water from which river? | 4
C The Liffey

In Manitoba, Canada, where is drinking forbidden? | 6
B In the toilet

What is the volume of a magnum? | 8
One third of a gallon

How did Krook, the gin-drinking, rag-and-bone man in Charles Dickens' Bleak House meet his bizarre end? | 10
He spontaneously combusted

2

A 'cosecha' is a drunk Italian prostitute. True or false?

4

What is a 'dargle'?
- **A** A pub
- **B** A discreet vomit
- **C** A swig of whisky

6

What happens to an ant if it gets drunk?
- **A** It explodes
- **B** It falls over onto its right side
- **C** It walks backwards and makes a slight hissing sound

8

Which Eric Clapton song is about a bloated rock star who is so drunk that his wife has to drive him home and undress him?

10

Why do some pewter English beermugs from the 18th century have glass bottoms?

10 – Questions

Which town is traditionally the centre of English brewing? **2**

In Egypt, drinking beer from a shoe is considered to be a cure for... **4**
- **A** A hangover
- **B** A broken heart
- **C** Malaria

In 1970, a drunken Japanese motorist managed to drive over a mile without... **6**
- **A** Realising he was in reverse
- **B** His recently-severed arm
- **C** Realising he had mistakenly climbed into a light aircraft

What does V.S.O.P. stand for? **8**

Which vegetable would the Egyptians rest on their foreheads to cure a hangover? **10**

2 *A 'cosecha' is a drunk Italian prostitute. True or false?*
False. It's a Spanish vintage

4 *What is a 'dargle'?*
A A pub

6 *What happens to an ant if it gets drunk?*
B It falls over onto its right side

8 *Which Eric Clapton song is about a bloated rock star who is so drunk that his wife has to drive him home and undress him?*
Wonderful Tonight

10 *Why do some pewter English beermugs from the 18th century have glass bottoms?*
Press gangs would slyly drop shillings into people's pint pots and when an unwitting drinker fished it out, they would claim he had "taken the king's shilling" and drag him off to the navy.
A glass-bottomed pot would prevent this

Which town is traditionally the centre of English brewing?

Burton on Trent

2

In Egypt, drinking beer from a shoe is considered to be a cure for...

B A broken heart

4

In 1970, a drunken Japanese motorist managed to drive over a mile without...

B His recently-severed arm

6

What does V.S.O.P. stand for?

Very Special Old Pale

8

Which vegetable would the Egyptians rest on their foreheads to cure a hangover?

A cabbage

10

2   *Johnson described claret as so weak "that a man would be drowned by it before it made him drunk". True or false?*

4   *The Manhattan cocktail was invented by...*
- **A**   Winston Churchill's mother
- **B**   F. Scott Fitzgerald's father
- **C**   Frank Sinatra's grandmother

6   *To 'eruct' means...*
- **A**   To filter wine
- **B**   To burp loudly
- **C**   To strengthen a beer after brewing

8   *Which actor plays Tom Cruise's boss in "Cocktail"?*

10   *Which popular drink has an English name derived from the Hebrew word 'shekar'?*

What drink does James Bond like "shaken, not stirred"?

2

Whose dying words were "Drink to me"?
- **A** Pablo Picasso
- **B** Dylan Thomas
- **C** Dorothy Parker

4

In bars in Saskatchaewan, it is illegal to...
- **A** Speak to other customers
- **B** Stand up and drink
- **C** Drink water

6

Which drink was known as 'blue ruin'?

8

Which actor plays Mickey Rourke and Matt Dillon's drunken father in "Rumblefish"?

10

2

Johnson described claret as so weak "that a man would be drowned by it before it made him drunk". True or false?
True

4

The Manhattan cocktail was invented by...
A Winston Churchill's mother

6

To 'eruct' means...
B To burp loudly

8

Which actor plays Tom Cruise's boss in "Cocktail"?
Bryan Brown

10

Which popular drink has an English name derived from the Hebrew word "shekar"?
Cider

What drink does James Bond like "shaken, not stirred"?
   A martini

2

Whose dying words were "Drink to me"?
   A Pablo Picasso

4

In bars in Saskatchaewan, it is illegal to...
   C Drink water

6

Which drink was known as 'blue ruin'?
   Gin, because of the colour it gave to the faces of its 18th century abusers

8

Which actor plays Mickey Rourke and Matt Dillon's drunken father in "Rumblefish"?
   Dennis Hopper

10

David Niven and Errol Flynn's Hollywood home was nicknamed "Cirrhosis By The Sea". True or false?

4

English Politician William Pitt (the Younger) was prescribed a bottle of port a day to cure his gout. How did he die?

A Drunkenly falling in front of a carriage
B From the pain of his gout
C Cirrhosis of the liver

6

Who said: "Always remember that I have taken more out of alcohol than alcohol has taken out of me."?

A P.J. O'Rourke
B J.F. Kennedy
C Winston Churchill

8

Where does the word 'Pils' come from?

10

Where does the word 'tiddly' meaning 'slightly drunk' come from?

In 1986, according to the Encyclopedia Americana, 2 million Americans were alcoholics. True or false?

2

In Australian drinking slang, what is a 'butcher'?
A A very small glass of beer (170ml)
B Someone with a voracious appetite for alcohol
C A cocktail of all the spirits on the bar

4

Which of these describe extreme drunkenness in Australia?
A As pissed as a possum
B As wrecked as a 'roo
C As drunk as Chloe

6

Where in the world is 'Moosehead' made?

8

What brewing ingredient is technically known as 'Humulus lupulus'?

10

2 *David Niven and Errol Flynn's Hollywood home was nicknamed "Cirrhosis By The Sea". True or false?*
   True

4 *English Politician William Pitt (the Younger) was prescribed a bottle of port a day to cure his gout. How did he die?*
   C   Cirrhosis of the liver

6 *Who said: "Always remember that I have taken more out of alcohol than alcohol has taken out of me."?*
   C   Winston Churchill

8 *Where does the word 'Pils' come from?*
   The town of Pilsn in the Czech Republic

10 *Where does the word 'tiddly' meaning 'slightly drunk' come from?*
   Tiddly wink, which rhymes with drink

In 1986, according to the Encyclopedia Americana, 2 million Americans were alcoholics. True or false?

2

False. The figure was 4 million

In Australian drinking slang, what is a 'butcher'?

4

A A very small glass of beer (170ml)

Which of these describe extreme drunkenness in Australia?

6

C As drunk as Chloe

Where in the world is 'Moosehead' made?

8

Canada

What brewing ingredient is technically known as 'Humulus lupulus'?

10

The common hop

2

In the court of Henry VIII, a page who made a handmaiden pregnant had his beer ration stopped for a month.
True or false?

4

According to the late Richard Burton, an alcoholic is someone who...

A Loves life so much he drinks himself to death

B Drinks more than his doctor

C Is hated by his friends for being able to drink more than them

6

Why did Ancient Greek drinkers wear wreaths?

B To show their relative drinking prowess

C As a mark of respect to the vine and to Bacchus

B To protect themselves from drink's noxious fumes

8

What is wrong with a German who is said to "need a herring"?

10

Where does Daiquiri Rum come from?

A firkin is...
- **A** 9 litres
- **B** 9 gallons
- **C** 9 pints

2

On German beer, what does 'hell' refer to?
- **A** Its relative bite
- **B** Its colour
- **C** Its brewing age

4

In 18th century England, what was a scuttlebutt?
- **A** A ship's water barrel
- **B** Someone who swept the tavern's floor in exchange for free drink
- **C** An enormous pewter beer jug, sufficient for a whole coach team

6

What distinguishes a French wine labelled 'agressif'?

8

Which British Prime Minister said: "I rather like bad wine...one gets so bored with good wine."?

10

2 _In the court of Henry VIII, a page who made a handmaiden pregnant would have his beer ration stopped for a month. True or false?_

    True

4 _According to the late Richard Burton, an alcoholic is someone who..._

    B Drinks more than his doctor

6 _Why did Ancient Greek drinkers wear wreaths?_

    C To protect themselves from drink's noxious fumes

8 _What is wrong with a German who is said to "need a herring"?_

    He has a hangover

10 _Where does Daiquiri Rum come from?_

    Cuba

A firkin is...
    B 9 gallons

2

On German beer, what does 'hell' refer to?
    B Its colour (It means 'light')

4

In 18th century England, what was a scuttlebutt?
    A A ship's water barrel

6

What distinguishes a French wine labelled 'agressif'?
    It's made from unripe grapes

8

Which British Prime Minister said: "I rather like bad wine...one gets so bored with good wine."?
    Benjamin Disraeli

10

2

The Sumerian goddess of drinking was called 'Burrpa'.
True or false?

4

W.C. Fields said: "A woman drove me to drink...
    A ...and then I drove her to Ohio. Seemed fair to me."
    B ...and I never even had the courtesy to thank her."
    C ...she dropped me off there, and I sure-as-hell ain't
        walking home."

6

What is a scuppernong?
    A A Maori name for an alcoholic drink
    B A type of white grape
    C An Anglo-Saxon drinking helmet

8

What is the highly toxic, fit-inducing ingredient of
absinthe that caused it to be banned in most European
countries?

10

In which year did Prohibition begin in the USA?

In 1911 Harry Houdini had to be rescued from a huge vat of Tetley's Beer. True or false?

2

In medieval England, what was an 'ale-conner'?
- **A** The lord's professional beer drinker and ale tester
- **B** Someone who would sell flavoured barley water in place of unfermented beer
- **C** A travelling master brewer

4

'Koeniglichbayerischeroberbiersteuerhaupteinkassierer' is a German word for...
- **A** A royal beer tax collector
- **B** A special royal "superior" beer
- **C** The German equivalent of "as drunk as a skunk"

6

Which country produces more beer than any other?

8

In which year did Prohibition in the USA end?

10

2 *The Sumerian goddess of drinking was called 'Burrpa'. True or false?*

False. Her name was Ninkasi

4 *W.C. Fields said: "A woman drove me to drink...*
  B ...and I never even had the courtesy to thank her."

6 *What is a scuppernong?*
  B A type of white grape

8 *What is the highly toxic, fit-inducing ingredient of absinthe that caused it to be banned in most European countries?*

Wormwood

10 *In which year did Prohibition begin in the USA?*
  1919

In 1911 Harry Houdini had to be rescued from a huge vat of Tetley's Beer. True or false?

> True. He had been challenged to perform an underwater escape in beer, but was unsurprisingly overcome by the alcohol

2

In medieval England, what was an 'ale-conner'?

> **A** The lord's professional beer drinker and ale tester

4

'Koeniglichbayerischeroberbiersteuerhaupteinkassierer' is a German word for...

> **A** A royal beer tax collector

6

Which country produces more beer than any other?

> USA

8

In which year did Prohibition in the USA end?

> 1933

10

2

Splodgenessabounds had chart success with "Two Pints of Lager And A Packet Of Crisps, Please". True or false?

4

Who owns the largest brewery in the world; Budweiser, Coors or Heineken?

6

Who said: "Give my people plenty of beer, good beer, and cheap beer, and you will have no revolution among them."?

- **A** Tsar Nicholas II
- **B** Fidel Castro
- **C** Queen Victoria

8

Which US president was killed whilst his valet, his coachman and his bodyguard were boozing?

10

Which thriller writer came up with the slogan "Guinness is good for you" whilst working in advertising?

Brewer's Droop had a surprise chart hit in the UK in 1974 with "Somerset Cider Inside Her." True or false?

2

In Australia, if you "drink with the flies", you...
- **A** Drink hardly anything
- **B** Drink alone
- **C** Drink anything you can get your hands on

4

In 1871, in the UK, what proportion of the adult population was involved in the production and distribution of alcohol?
- **A** 0.04%
- **B** 2%
- **C** 8%

6

Which biblical character had to be dressed by his son after flooding himself with wine?

8

Grappa is an Italian form of brandy. How does it differ from normal brandy?

10

2   *Splodgenessabounds had chart success with "Two Pints of Lager And A Packet Of Crisps, Please". True or false?*

True

4   *Who owns the largest brewery in the world; Budweiser, Coors or Heineken?*

Coors. Its plant in Colorado produces over 2.2 billion litres of beer a year

6   *Who said: "Give my people plenty of beer, good beer, and cheap beer, and you will have no revolution among them."?*

C   Queen Victoria

8   *Which US president was killed whilst his valet, his coachman and his bodyguard were boozing?*

Abraham Lincoln

10   *Which thriller writer came up with the slogan "Guinness is good for you" whilst working in advertising?*

Dorothy L. Sayers

Brewer's Droop had a surprise chart hit in the UK in 1974 with "Somerset Cider Inside Her." True or false?

2

False

In Australia, if you "drink with the flies", you...

4

B Drink alone

In 1871, in the UK, what proportion of the adult population was involved in the production and distribution of alcohol?

6

C 8%

Which biblical character had to be dressed by his son after flooding himself with wine?

8

Noah

Grappa is an Italian form of brandy. How does it differ from normal brandy?

10

It's made from the skins, stalks and pips, rather than the grapes themselves

2

Beer and wine contain ethanol, while spirits contain methyl alcohol. True or false?

4

W.C. Fields claimed he never drank "anything stronger than _____ before breakfast."

A Beer
B Gin
C Sherry

6

How did Barry Humphries describe being sick?

A Painting the town red (and yellow and green and brown)
B Enjoying yourself in reverse
C A colourful way to say goodnight

8

Which Japanese city is sake originally from?

10

What is the connection between armagnac and birth control?

'Bastard' was an 18th century name for claret.
True or false?

2

In medieval England, the lord's beer tester would check if
ale was of good quality by...

A Pouring a pint over his head, then burning his hair and
examining the flame

B Making his dog and/or apprentice drink half a gallon to see
the effects

C Pouring a pint on a chair and then sitting in it wearing leather
trousers (if he didn't stick after half an hour, it wasn't
strong enough)

4

Which English monarch regularly breakfasted on a
quart of ale?

A Elizabeth I

B Edward VII

C William of Orange

6

Which drink is mentioned several times in Hemingway's
"For Whom the Bells Toll" for its erotic powers?

8

Why was the famous pirate Captain Kidd's
execution delayed?

10

2

Beer and wine contain ethanol, while spirits contain methyl alcohol. True or false?

False. All alcoholic drinks contain ethanol only. Methyl alcohol is highly toxic

4

W.C. Fields claimed he never drank "anything stronger than _____ before breakfast."

B Gin

6

How did Barry Humphries describe being sick?

B Enjoying yourself in reverse

8

Which Japanese city is sake originally from?

Osaka (hence the name)

10

What is the connection between armagnac and birth control?

The commercial centre of the Armagnac region, in France, is called Condom

'Bastard' was an 18th century name for claret.
True or false?

2

False. It was actually a 17th century tawny wine

In medieval England, the lord's beer tester would check if
ale was of good quality by...

   C Pouring a pint on a chair and then sitting in it wearing leather
trousers (if he didn't stick after half an hour, it wasn't
strong enough)

4

Which English monarch regularly breakfasted on a
quart of ale?

   A Elizabeth I

6

Which drink is mentioned several times in Hemingway's
"For Whom the Bell Tolls" for its erotic powers?

   Absinthe

8

Why was the famous pirate Captain Kidd's
execution delayed?

   Because the executioner was too drunk to stand up

10

2

In 1599, the commander of the English navy entertained 6,000 guests with punch served by waiters floating in a punch bowl. True or false?

4

In 16th century England, drunkards were forced, as a punishment, to parade around the town in the 'Newcastle Jacket'. It was...

   A A lidless barrel with a headhole cut in the base
   B A hessian sack filled with fish scraps and vegetables
   C A heavy wooden placard reading "I am an accursed drinker and am thus mine own damnation."

6

Which country produces most wine?

   A Italy
   B France
   C USA

8

Pernod, Ricard and Berger are all brand names of a certain kind of spirit. What is its name?

10

How many firkins in a butt?

A Hail Mary is a Bloody Mary made with hail instead of ice. True or false?

2

What is a 'God-forbid-me'?
- **A** A very strong beer, brewed for one day a year by Franciscan friars
- **B** A mixture of rum, gin and sour milk, used as a morning-after "never again" cure
- **C** An enormous two-handled drinking mug

4

In Ireland in 1978, what percentage of the price of whiskey was the cost of producing the whiskey itself?
- **A** 3%
- **B** 23%
- **C** 63%

6

Of whom is the following true: "Some drink to remember, some drink to forget."?

8

What should you drink because "you deserve what every individual should enjoy regularly"?

10

2 In 1599, the commander of the English navy entertained 6,000 guests with punch served by waiters floating in a punch bowl. True or false?

True

4 In 16th century England, drunkards were forced, as a punishment, to parade around the town in the 'Newcastle Jacket'. It was...

A A lidless barrel with a headhole cut in the base

6 Which country produces most wine?

A Italy

8 Pernod, Ricard and Berger are all brand names of a certain kind of spirit. What is its name?

Pastis

10 How many firkins in a butt?

12. A firkin is 9 gallons, a butt 108 gallons

A Hail Mary is a Bloody Mary made with hail instead of ice. True or false?
> False

2

What is a 'God-forbid-me'?
> **C** An enormous two-handled drinking mug

4

In Ireland in 1978, what percentage of the price of whiskey was the cost of producing the whiskey itself?
> **A** 3%

6

Of whom is the following true: "Some drink to remember, some drink to forget."?
> The residents of "Hotel California", by The Eagles

8

What should you drink because "you deserve what every individual should enjoy regularly"?
> Budweiser

10

2 *Irish Coffee was invented at Shannon airport. True or false?*

4 *Which country drinks most beer per head?*
- **A** America
- **B** New Zealand
- **C** The UK

6 *Which of the following is early American slang for liquor?*
- **A** Tooth-rot
- **B** Cheek-blush
- **C** Nose-paint

8 *What part of a wine bottle is the 'punt'?*

10 *If someone proposes a toast with "no heel taps", what do you have to do?*

Which of these is Australian slang for a beer?
A A freezer
B A frozen tube
C An ice cold

2

How did Dylan Thomas define an alcoholic?
A Someone you don't like who drinks as much as you
B Someone who sees nothing but horror in an empty bottle
C Someone with a mortal fear of hangovers

4

With which country would you associate beers with names meaning Sun, Crown and Two Xs?

6

Alcoholics are sometimes given 'chemical fences'. What are they?

8

What is the most popular beer brewed by the Archipelago Brewing Company in Kuala Lumpur?

10

2 › *Irish Coffee was invented at Shannon airport. True or false?*

  True

---

4 › *Which country drinks most beer per head?*

  B New Zealand

---

6 › *Which of the following is early American slang for liquor?*

  C Nose-paint

---

8 › *What part of a wine bottle is the 'punt'?*

  The hollow in its base

---

10 › *If someone proposes a toast with "no heel taps", what do you have to do?*

  Down it in one go

Which of these is Australian slang for a beer?
   C   An ice cold
> 2

How did Dylan Thomas define an alcoholic?
   A   Someone you don't like who drinks as much as you
> 4

With which country would you associate beers with names meaning Sun, Crown and Two Xs?
   Mexico. Sol, Corona and Dos Equis
> 6

Alcoholics are sometimes given 'chemical fences'. What are they?
   Drugs that react with alcohol to induce nausea
> 8

What is the most popular beer brewed by the Archipelago Brewing Company in Kuala Lumpur?
   ABC beer
> 10

2

During the reign of Catherine I of Russia, why were the Moscow ballrooms filled with women dressed as men?

4

What is the name given to someone who collects beer-bottle labels?

   A   A labologist

   B   A squeerologist

   C   A labelarian

6

What does 'crapulent' mean?

   A   Weak bladdered

   B   Prone to sadness when drinking

   C   Frequently indulging in alcohol

8

Which country's largest whisky company is called 'Suntory'?

10

What does a 'tegestologist' collect?

What was the name of the Hofmeister bear?

2

Complete the following piece of bar room wisdom from Cheers' Norm: "Women; can't live with them;...
- **A** ...can't live without them."
- **B** ...don't want to."
- **C** ...pass the beer nuts."

4

The Etruscan god of wine was called...
- **A** Nurrlik
- **B** Fufluns
- **C** Nasti

6

Richter, Sykes and Cartier are methods of doing what?

8

In which country is 'Pripps' the giant in the beer industry?

10

2 > *During the reign of Catherine I of Russia, why were the Moscow ballrooms filled with women dressed as men?*
Women were banned from getting drunk

4 > *What is the name given to someone who collects beer-bottle labels?*
A A labologist

6 > *What does 'crapulent' mean?*
C Frequently indulging in alcohol

8 > *Which country's largest whisky company is called 'Suntory'?*
Japan's

10 > *What does a 'tegestologist' collect?*
Beer mats

What was the name of the Hofmeister bear?
George

2

Complete the following piece of bar room wisdom from Cheers' Norm: "Women; can't live with them;...
C ...pass the beer nuts."

4

The Etruscan god of wine was called...
B Fufluns

6

Richter, Sykes and Cartier are methods of doing what?
Measuring alcoholic content

8

In which country is 'Pripps' the giant in the beer industry?
Sweden

10

2 *What did the Americans mean by 'coffin varnish'?*

4 *The word 'hooch' comes from the Hoochino people.*
Where do they come from?
- **A** Iceland
- **B** Alaska
- **C** Siberia

6 *From which novel does the following come from:*
"Those were drinking days and most men drank hard"?
- **A** "The Sun Also Rises" by Ernest Hemingway
- **B** "The Big Sleep" by Raymond Chandler
- **C** "A Tale of Two Cities" by Charles Dickens

8 *Joe E. Lewis said: "I distrust _____ and anyone else*
who can go a week without a drink." Who or what?

10 *What is the name for a barrel six times as big as*
a firkin?

What cocktail is named after the Californian surfer Tom Harvey because of his behaviour when he was drunk?

2

Does 'punch' takes its name from an old Indian word meaning 'house','drunk' or 'five'?

4

Which of the following is not a real French wine?
   A Le Pis
   B Les Migraines
   C Chateau Cilla

6

Which British beer is often known as 'The Dog'?

8

What is 'zymurgy'?

10

2 *What did the Americans mean by 'coffin varnish'?*
Liquor

4 *The word 'hooch' comes from the Hoochino people. Where do they come from?*
B Alaska

6 *From which novel does the following come from: "Those were drinking days and most men drank hard"?*
C "A Tale of Two Cities" by Charles Dickens

8 *Joe E. Lewis said: "I distrust _____ and anyone else who can go a week without a drink." Who or what?*
Camels

10 *What is the name for a barrel six times as big as a firkin?*
A hogshead

What cocktail is named after the Californian surfer Tom Harvey because of his behaviour when he was drunk? 2

The Harvey Wallbanger

Does 'punch' takes its name from an old Indian word meaning 'house', 'drunk' or 'five'? 4

Five, the number of ingredients originally thought necessary

Which of the following is not a real French wine? 6

C Chateau Cilla

Which British beer is often known as 'The Dog'? 8

Newcastle Brown Ale — from the habit of Newcastle men, claiming they were just going out "to walk the dog"

What is 'zymurgy'? 10

The art and science of brewing

2 *The word "sherry" comes from the Spanish region of Jerez. True or false?*

4 *To commemorate the tricentenary of his death, the Japanese produced a batch of Mozart K.001 sake. To make it special...*

    A The fermentation vat contained wood from a clavichord once owned by Mozart

    B Two of Mozart's descendants participated in the rice-stirring ceremony

    C A selection of Mozart's work was played to assist the fermentation

6 *What is an acetobacter?*

    A A gland that controls alcohol levels in the brain

    B A wine vat sterilizer

    C A bacterium that turns wine to vinegar

8 *What is 'the Amber Nectar'?*

10 *Gin used to be called 'geneva'. Which country does it come from?*

At one time it was thought that carrying the ashes of the burnt livers of frogs and hedgehogs in a bag would cure alcohol-induced sexual impotence. True or false?

2

Richard Burton plays a brooding alcoholic in the film "Come Back, Little Sheba". True or false?

4

What is a 'fob'?

- **A** The froth, or head, on beer
- **B** A traditional Dutch drinking bib
- **C** A 16th century word for a portly drunkard

6

What is balderdash?

8

What does 'Drambuie' mean?

10

2 > *The word "sherry" comes from the Spanish region of Jerez. True or false?*
True

4 > *To commemorate the tricentenary of his death, the Japanese produced a batch of Mozart K.001 sake. To make it special...*
C A selection of Mozart's work was played to assist the fermentation

6 > *What is an acetobacter?*
C A bacterium that turns wine to vinegar

8 > *What is 'the Amber Nectar'?*
Fosters lager

10 > *Gin used to be called 'geneva'. Which country does it come from?*
Holland. 'Jenever' is Dutch for 'juniper'

At one time it was thought that carrying the ashes of the burnt livers of frogs and hedgehogs in a bag would cure alcohol-induced sexual impotence. True or false?

2

True

Richard Burton played a brooding alcoholic in the film "Come Back, Little Sheba." True or false?

4

False. Burt Lancaster did

What is a 'fob'?

6

A the froth, or head, on beer. (To "fob someone off" is thus to give them something insufficient or sub-standard)

What is balderdash?

8

Any strange and unpleasant mixture of drinks e.g. milk and beer

What does 'Drambuie' mean?

10

Golden drink

2

In the 19th century, swallowing ammonia was a popular hangover cure. True or false?

4

'Eck' is...
   A Sediment in cask ale
   B A German vineyard
   C "Cheers" in Innuit

6

Arrack is an aniseed spirit, similar to ouzo. What does 'arrack' mean in Arabic?
   A The water that cleanses
   B Sweat
   C Mother's milk

8

What is the top selling beer in the world?

10

In the 1950s, the French wine estate of Chateauneuf Du Pape forbade what sort of trespass?

Why should champagne glasses always be completely dry?

How did Sultan Suliman I punish persistent drunkards?
- **A** He would have them ducked repeatedly in a vat of sour wine
- **B** He tattooed "I am a demon" on their foreheads
- **C** He poured molten lead down their throats

In 1735, the British annual gin consumption was...
- **A** 400,000 gallons
- **B** 1,700,000 gallons
- **C** 11,000,000 gallons

Who, when driven to drink by a beautiful blonde, remarked: "It's the one thing I'm indebted to her for."?

In "Animal House", what is the name of John Belushi's character, who downs a bottle of bourbon in one draught?

2 *In the 19th century, swallowing ammonia was a popular hangover cure. True or false?*
   True

4 *'Eck' is...*
   B A German vineyard

6 *Arrack is an aniseed spirit, similar to ouzo. What does 'arrack' mean in Arabic?*
   B Sweat

8 *What is the top selling beer in the world?*
   Budweiser

10 *In the 1950s, the French wine estate of Chateauneuf Du Pape forbade against what sort of trespass?*
   Trespass by UFOs

Why should champagne glasses always be completely dry?
Any wetness kills the bubbles

2

How did Sultan Suliman I punish persistent drunkards?
  C He poured molten lead down their throats

4

In 1735, the British annual gin consumption was...
  C 11,000,000 gallons

6

Who, when driven to drink by a beautiful blonde, remarked: "It's the one thing I'm indebted to her for."?
W.C. Fields

8

In "Animal House", what is the name of John Belushi's character, who downs a bottle of bourbon in one draught?
Bluto

10

2 "Whip and Tongue" is a bar of ill-repute in Manhattan. True or false?

4 'Pimpeltjens' is a word of Dutch origin. It is...
  A A pus-coloured liqueur
  B The traditional Dutch barman's apron
  C The name of an alcoholic foreign secretary who disgraced himself on national TV

6 Where does the word "boozer" come from?
  A The East End of London
  B Egypt
  C India

8 Which well-known drink has an original gravity of 1,000?

10 What was special about the WWII ship HMS Menesthus?

Bastardo and Spanna are both types of Madeira.
True or false?

2

Who said: "I'd hate to be a teetotaler. Imagine getting up
in the morning and knowing that's as good as you're
going to feel all day."?

4

   A Dean Martin
   B Keith Richards
   C Elvis Presley

In 1989 what was the average annual beer consumption
per head in the UK?

6

   A 21.9 litres
   B 110.4 litres
   C 967.1 litres

If you've had 'a sniff of the barman's apron', you are
thought to do what?

8

Which film about a drinker won the best actor and best
picture Oscars in 1946?

10

2

"Whip and Tongue" is a bar of ill-repute in Manhattan. True or false?

False. It's a method of grafting vines, popular with French viticulturists

4

'Pimpeltjens' is a word of Dutch origin. It is...

A A pus-coloured liqueur

6

Where does the word "boozer" come from?

B Egypt. (Reports of an "abominable liquor" of this name reached the UK in 1852)

8

Which well-known drink has an original gravity of 1.000?

Water

10

What was special about the WWII ship HMS Menesthus?

In 1945, it was converted into a floating military brewery

Bastardo and Spanna are both types of Madeira.
True or false?

> 2

False. Bastardo is, but Spanna is an Italian wine

Who said: "I'd hate to be a teetotaler. Imagine getting up
in the morning and knowing that's as good as you're
going to feel all day."?

> 4

A Dean Martin

In 1989 what was the average annual beer consumption
per head in the UK?

> 6

B 110.4 litres

If you've had 'a sniff of the barman's apron', you are
thought to do what?

> 8

Get drunk very easily

Which film about a drinker won the best actor and best
picture Oscars in 1946?

> 10

The Lost Weekend

2

'Heaven under the Arches' is a mixture of rum, vodka and gold dust. True or false?

4

What year did Guinness start brewing?
- **A** 1698
- **B** 1759
- **C** 1807

6

Which amendment to the US Constitution banned liquor?
- **A** The 5th
- **B** The 9th
- **C** The 18th

8

Which famous spirit company was taken over by Cuba's Fidel Castro in 1960?

10

How is Guinness connected with Australian James Bond star, George Lazenby?

In the 18th century, the ordinary working man's allowance of beer was a gallon each working day. True or false?

2

Complete this old English proverb: "Good ale will make a cat...
- **A** ...speak."
- **B** ...bark."
- **C** ...bad ale will make a rat."

4

Most beer is clarified with a substance extracted from...
- **A** Pigs' kidneys
- **B** Sheep's pancreases
- **C** Fish's air bladders

6

In "MASH", what was Radar's favourite drink?

8

What do whisky, aquavit and vodka have in common?

10

2 > 'Heaven under the Arches' is a mixture of rum, vodka and gold dust. True or false?

False

4 > *What year did Guinness start brewing?*

B 1759

6 > *Which amendment to the US Constitution banned liquor?*

C The 18th

8 > *Which famous spirit company was taken over by Cuba's Fidel Castro in 1960?*

Bacardi

10 > *How is Guinness connected with Australian James Bond star, George Lazenby?*

Lazenby's only Bond film was "On Her Majesty's Secret Service", which featured Louis Armstrong singing "All The Time In The World", a song later used in a Guinness advertisement

In 1814, a huge storage vat of porter (a bitter beer brewed from charred or browned malt, originally made especially for porters) exploded in Liquorpond Street, London, destroying three houses and killing eight people. True or false?

Which film contains the immortal line: "Fat, drunk and stupid is no way to go through life, son."?
- **A** Animal House
- **B** Planes, Trains and Automobiles
- **C** Carry On At Your Convenience

When was lager first brewed in Britain?
- **A** 1301
- **B** 1879
- **C** 1929

Which US city is "The Blues Brothers" set in?

According to Scott Fitzgerald, what time of night is "the real dark night of the soul"?

2 | *'Gemima Puddleduck' is Australian slang for a man with a weak bladder. True or false?*
False

4 | *Which organisation was responsible for making beer in metal kegs popular in the UK?*
C The US Air Force

6 | *Which country imports most champagne in total per year?*
A UK

8 | *What is 'ebriosity'?*
Habitual drunkenness

10 | *Why does the English Navy refer to rum as 'Nelson's blood'?*
After Trafalgar, Nelson's body was shipped home in a cask of rum, which was afterwards returned to service

In 1814, a huge storage vat of porter exploded on Liquorpond Street, London, destroying three houses and killing eight people. True or false?

> True

2

Which film contains the immortal line: "Fat, drunk and stupid is no way to go through life, son."?

> **A** Animal House

4

When was lager first brewed in Britain?

> **B** 1879

6

Which US city is "The Blues Brothers" set in?

> Chicago

8

According to Scott Fitzgerald, what time of night is "the real dark night of the soul"?

> Three in the morning

10

2

In 17th century hospitals, children were given two gallons of beer a week. True or false?

4

When did canned beer first appear in Britain?
- **A** 1936
- **B** 1955
- **C** 1962

6

'Ullage' is...
- **A** A single malt from the Outer Hebrides
- **B** The distance between the wine and the cork in a bottle
- **C** A dry white French wine similar to Medoc

8

In which country did alcohol-free lager originate?

10

Why did Graham Greene never drink liqueurs?

The film "Ice Cold In Alex" is named after the promise of a cold beer. True or false?

2

Critic and wit Dorothy Parker said: "One more drink and I'll be under...

A ...the table."

B ...the carpet."

C ...the host."

4

Which brand of beer can clearly be seen in Manet's painting "The Bar at the Folies Bergeres"?

A Heineken

B Bass

C Lowenbrau

6

Who recorded the original version of "Red Red Wine"?

8

In the Peter Sellers Cold War comedy "Dr Strangelove", why will Col. Ripper mix only rainwater with his bourbon?

10

2 In 17th century hospitals, children were given two gallons of beer a week. True or false?

True. Beer was cleaner and safer than water

4 When did canned beer first appear in Britain?

A 1936

6 'Ullage' is...

B The distance between the wine and the cork in a bottle

8 In which country did alcohol-free lager originate?

Switzerland

10 Why did Graham Greene never drink liqueurs?

Because another writer told him that 'serious writers' didn't drink them

The film "Ice Cold In Alex" is named after the promise of a cold beer. True or false?

2

    True

Critic and wit Dorothy Parker said: "One more drink and I'll be under...

4

    C ...the host."

Which brand of beer can clearly be seen in Manet's painting "The Bar at the Folies Bergeres"?

6

    B Bass

Who recorded the original version of "Red Red Wine"?

8

    Neil Diamond

In the Peter Sellers Cold War comedy "Dr Strangelove", why will Col. Ripper mix only rainwater with his bourbon?

10

    He believes that fluoridation of tap water is a communist mind-control plot

2

What is called 'wailing of cats' in Germany, 'wailing of kittens' in Poland and 'carpenters' in Denmark?

4

Zwack Unicum is...
- **A** The man who introduced the Pilsn method of lager brewing to America
- **B** An Italian herbal liqueur
- **C** The bacteria that decimated French white-grape vineyards in the 1970s

6

What is a 'posset'?
- **A** A skilled hop-grader or "tickler"
- **B** A mixture of egg, milk and beer or wine
- **C** A barmaid's money pouch

8

Which US city is "Cheers" set in?

10

Which writer does Mickey Rourke play in the film "Barfly"?

An 'East & West' cocktail consists of sherry mixed with vodka. True or false?

2

A 'shive' is...
- **A** A wooden beer tap
- **B** A vent in a beer barrel
- **C** An 18th century drunkard

4

What is the world's best selling brand of scotch?

6

What powder was originally used to test the proof of alcohol?

8

What is the main ingredient of gin?

10

2 > *What is called 'wailing of cats' in Germany, 'wailing of kittens' in Poland and 'carpenters' in Denmark?*
A hangover

4 > *Zwack Unicum is...*
B An Italian herbal liqueur

6 > *What is a 'posset'?*
B A mixture of egg, milk and beer or wine

8 > *Which US city is "Cheers" set in?*
Boston

10 > *Which writer does Mickey Rourke play in the film "Barfly"?*
Charles Bukowski

An 'East & West' cocktail consists of sherry mixed with vodka. True or false?

2

True

A 'shive' is...

4

B A vent in a beer barrel

What is the world's best selling brand of scotch?

6

Johnnie Walker

What powder was originally used to test the proof of alcohol?

8

Gunpowder

What is the main ingredient of gin?

10

Grain

SOME OF THE TITLES AVAILABLE FROM LAGOON BOOKS:

MIND-BENDING PUZZLE BOOKS

Cont...

Mind-Bending Conundrums & Puzzles	ISBN 1899712038
Mind-Bending Classic Logic Puzzles	ISBN 1899712186
Mind-Bending Classic Word Puzzles	ISBN 1899712054
Mind-Bending Crossword Puzzles	ISBN 1899712399

MYSTERY PUZZLE BOOKS

Death After Dinner	ISBN 1899712461
Murder On The Riviera Express	ISBN 189971247X
Murder in Manhattan	ISBN 1899712488
Death In The Family	ISBN 1899712496
60 Second Murder Mystery Puzzles	ISBN 1899712453

All books can be ordered from bookshops by quoting the above ISBN number.